3-Short

A Trio of Short Plays

By Gabriel Davis

gabriel@alumni.cmu.edu
gabrielbdavis.com

Un-Chatty Cathy

10 Minute Play

By Gabriel Davis

gabriel@alumni.cmu.edu
gabrielbdavis.com

Cast
2 w, 1 m

Characters
Cathy
Patsy
Zachary

All are teenagers in high school.

Time & Settings
Present Day. High School cafeteria at lunchtime.   Zachary's
locker right after lunch.

(Lunchtime at the school cafeteria. Cathy and Patsy are sitting, food mostly finished on their trays. Patsy has her phone camera pointed at Cathy who is finishing a carton of milk or juice. Behind them is a large screen on which we can see what Patsy is recording on her phone camera as video footage. A closeup of Cathy fills the large screen. Cathy looks over at Patsy).

CATHY

What are you doing?

PATSY

I'm making a reality show.

CATHY

Stop it, Patsy.

PATSY

It's called The Wallflower. It's about a girl looking for love. But she goes on zero dates. So she finds zero love.

CATHY

Press Pause on Reality.

(Patsy freezes. It's as if time has actually stopped. The image of Cathy on the large screen behind them has also paused. Cathy herself on stage is the only one not frozen. Cathy addresses the audience)

CATHY

Don't you wish you could do that? Just tell reality to take a chill pill for a second? So you can think for a second about what you want to say or do?
(Cathy gestures toward the image of herself on screen)

4

That's me. Cathy. In a moment I'll bury my head in my
notebook and begin drawing kittens. That's what I tend to do
in reality when I'm faced with a challenging situation. At
home I have a shelf of notebooks filled with kittens. I wish I
would do something else here.
>(Gestures toward Patsy)
That's Patsy. You could say we've known each other since age
zero. Our moms met at a MyGym Music Together class when
we were newborns. Our moms have been the best of friends
ever since. And they insist that we're the best of friends too.
>(Beat)
Play Reality.
>(Time unfreezes. The image of Cathy on the screen is
>now active as is Patsy holding the phone still pointed at
>Cathy. Cathy takes a notebook out of her backpack and
>begins sketching in it)

PATSY

Here's the moment where The Wallflower finally talks to the
man of her dreams!

CATHY

Turn it off.

PATSY

C'mon Cathy.

CATHY

I'm serious.

PATSY

>(Mocking)
I'm serious.

CATHY

Pause. She's talking about Zachary.

He's a regional spelling bee champion, he's on the chess club and he plays basketball. You could say he's a Renaissance man. Or a Renaissance boy I guess. I have had a crush on him since the 7th grade. But I've never even spoken to him. When we started high school we were assigned to the same homeroom. My assigned seat is directly behind his.
(Beat)
Play Reality.

                    PATSY
If you won't go over there and talk to him I will.

                    CATHY
Pause Reality. Patsy's always been more outgoing than me. She has Civics class with Zachary's best friend Brett who told her that Zachary wants to ask me to the Spring dance. And ever since she heard that she's been obsessed with me talking to him. Play Reality.

                    PATSY
            (Talking to her "audience" on the phone camera. She
            might alternate here between video selfie and pointing
            camera back at Cathy)
Yes ladies and gentleman. The Wallflower, too scared to talk to the man of her dreams, buries her head in her notebook of cats. Will The Wallflower walk over and say hello to Zachary right now or will she miss her one chance at love and be fated to forever draw cats and perhaps someday buy actual cats and live with those cats and be a cat lady?

                    CATHY
I will talk to him.

                    PATSY
When?

6

CATHY

Soon.

PATSY

Soon as in now?

CATHY

Soon as in soon.

PATSY
(Talking to her "audience" again on the video)
Yes, this is the moment in The Wallflower where it becomes clear our poor Wallflower is going to let her one chance at love pass her by. Forever alone. Cue the violins!

CATHY

Pause. I will talk to Zachary. I just have to figure out what I'm going to say first. And how I'm going to say it. Play.
(To Patsy)
Whatever, Patsy.

PATSY

Seriously, Cath... The Spring Dance is basically tomorrow.

CATHY

Pause. The Spring Dance is over a month away. So I found a public speaking class online. I'm studying every night and preparing my words. Play.
(To Patsy)
There's plenty of time.

PATSY

Is there? Most people already know who they're going to the dance with except for us Cathy.

Do you even know how lucky you are? A boy, a cute, smart boy likes you and wants to ask you to the dance and all you have to do is go over there and say "hi" and he will ask you. And then at least one of us will go to the dance and not be a total loser.

                              CATHY
You'll find a date.

                              PATSY
Brett already has a date. Tiffany Sanders locked him in back in January. And the only other boy I'm even remotely interested in likes you.

                              CATHY
You like Zachary?

                              PATSY
But you have dibs. Because you're my friend. So, like, go over there. Now. Or I will.

                              CATHY
Pause Reality.

                              PATSY
What are you saying?

                              CATHY
Why isn't it working? Pause Reality! Pause Reality!

                              PATSY
Fine. Whatever. I'm doing it. I'm going over there!

                              CATHY
Pause Reality! Pause Reality!

(Patsy Exits)

CATHY

But you can't pause reality you know?
    (She pulls out index cards and begins writing on them)
It just keeps whizzing past you at the speed of reality and it
never stops and you'll never be totally prepared for it so
sometimes you just have to take what you already are and go
with that and take a leap of faith that what you are right now
will be enough.
    (Puts index cards in her bag)
Here I go!

    (Lights up on Patsy talking to Zachary at another table
    in the cafeteria)

PATSY

…. that's just how she feels. I'm sorry. It's a lost cause.

ZACHARY

    (Clearly upset)
I'm out of here!
    (Exits quickly, maybe sobbing a little)

CATHY

What happened?

PATSY

Cathy! You came over.
    (To her "audience" on camera)
Ladies and Gentleman, you saw it here first, a small step for
Cathy, a giant leap for Wallflower-kind!

CATHY

What did you say?

PATSY

I'm so proud of you.

CATHY

Did you actually ask him to the dance?

PATSY

I didn't think you ever would. That's the only reason why.

CATHY

So now you're going with him?

PATSY

No that jerk said he only had eyes for you and he told me
"no." So I told him he should give up on that idea because
you were never going to come over here because you think
he's ugly because the acne medicine isn't working and that he
smells like old socks.

CATHY

Why would you say that?

PATSY

He rejected me. I was mad. It just came to me. Zing, right?

CATHY

I can't believe you!

PATSY

It's actually a good thing for your reality show.

CATHY

Enough with the show!   There is no show!

PATSY

But I got video editing software and everything. And now, thanks to me, the show has real dramatic stakes. Now he's heartbroken and probably angry at you.
    (Talking to her "audience" on camera)
Who knows if he'll say yes? Will he or won't he? Find out in tonight's episode of The Wallflower.

    (Cathy begins to exit. Patsy follows her recording the action on her phone)

CATHY

Don't follow me.

    (They weave around the stage, as if moving through hallways in the school)

PATSY
    (Narrating for the camera)
Her courage up, The Wallflower takes off to face her biggest fear and her greatest dream: Zachary!
    (To Patsy)
His locker is the other way.

    (Cathy changes direction)

CATHY

I don't need your help.

PATSY
What are best friends for? You're welcome!
    (To Camera, continuing to follow Cathy)
Like a shy panther she stalks her prey! Finally she spots him, standing at his locker.
    (Lights up on Zachary at a locker)
Now is her moment!
    (Getting in Zachary's face with camera)

Oooh he looks mad. Will he accept this Wallflower?
        (Moving camera back to Cathy)
We're about to find out!!!!

                        CATHY

Go away!

                        ZACHARY

Hey …

                        CATHY

Hello, hi … hello.

                        ZACHARY

Hey.

        (Overly long pause)

                        CATHY
        (Bursts out, maybe overly loud)
I'm Cathy!
        (Pulls it back a bit)
I'm not a chatty Cathy. I'm an un-chatty Cathy.
        (Laughs weakly at her joke)
That's why I'm taking a public speaking class. They say,
break the ice with a personal anecdote. Would you ... excuse
us, Patsy?
        (Patsy backs away, still recording Cathy and Zachary's
        Exchange on her phone. Throughout the following,
        Patsy creeps back toward them)
When I was six, I was a bluebird in the Camp Fire Girls of
America and had to sell cookies door to door. My older
brother laughed. "How is she gonna sell them? She never
makes a peep!"

I could feel my eyes getting a little wet. My mother got quiet and took out a pen and index card. She said, write your words. I wrote: "Hello, my name is Cathy. How would you like to purchase some cookies to benefit the Campfire Girls of America?" She smiled, "Now fly, my little bluebird!" To my brother she said "You're going to take her."

We went door to door. When someone opened, I'd find myself un-chatty. But I had my words! I'd hold out my card! I sold every box.

I wanted to tell you that because sometimes you have the words, but it's hard to voice them. I know you were going to ask me something. But then Patsy said I think you're funny lookin' cause your acne medicine isn't working. Well I didn't say those words. But I DID write these!

> (Holds up a large index card. "Patsy is a Jerk." And then "You're cute." And finally "Be My Dance Date." Patsy is quite close to them again now, so the audience can clearly see what's written on each card)

What do you say? I have a blank card and a pen, if that'd be easier for you.

PATSY
(Awkwardly close to Zachary with her phone)
Well Zachary ... will you accept this Wallflower?

> (Zachary holds the index card Cathy gave him. It says "Yes". Patsy has circled around Zachary to get the right angle on his index card)

CATHY
Pause Reality.

(Zachary and Patsy freeze. The image of Zachary on screen also freezes of him holding up the index card with "Yes.")

And for a moment it works again. But this time I'm not pausing it to think about what I'm going to do next. I'm pausing it to appreciate it. This is the moment where a dream and reality intersect. And I want to just be here in this moment a little longer. So I can remember it and return to it. And make more moments like this again.

(Beat)

Play reality.

(Blackout)

END OF PLAY

Stranger

10 Minute Play

By Gabriel Davis

gabriel@alumni.cmu.edu
gabrielbdavis.com

Cast
1 w, 1 m

Characters
Jocelyn
Man

Both characters are in their early twenties.

Time & Setting
Present day. A coffee shop in New York City.

(Jocelyn is looking around the coffee shop for an open seat. She spots one at a two seat table where a man is reading *The Stranger* by Albert Camus)

                    JOCELYN
Hi there.

                    MAN
Hi.

                    JOCELYN
The Stranger?

                    MAN
Oh...yeah. Favorite book.

                    JOCELYN
Really? Why?

                    MAN
It's very accurate.

                    JOCELYN
Can I have this seat?

                    MAN
Can you?

                    JOCELYN
It's just – this is the only open seat....

                    MAN
That's New York City. First time here?

JOCELYN

Yes.

MAN

It shows.

JOCELYN

Really? I kept telling myself no one would know I was really from Iowa if I just acted like I knew where I was going. But this little voice in my head was saying "everyone knows" you don't look like a city girl, you don't walk like a city girl, they're all looking at you, they all know you don't belong. But I figured I was just being paranoid.

MAN

Nope. No. Those primal feelings are usually right on point.

JOCELYN

So can I sit here?

MAN

I'm really not comfortable with strangers.

JOCELYN

Oh...ok.
		(Jocelyn begins to move away)

MAN

Waiit. I was being...ironic?

JOCELYN

Oh...the book. Right.

MAN

Sit. Please.

                    JOCELYN
Thanks. You actually like that book?

                    MAN
I actually do.

                    JOCELYN
I kinda thought it was a load of crap.

                    MAN
Wow. Nice opener. I just let you have that seat.

                    JOCELYN
Please. I may be from Iowa, but you didn't let me do anything. I
could have just taken it.

                    MAN
This is a new side of you.

                    JOCELYN
I was being polite before. And I knew if I walked away...you'd offer
the seat.

                    MAN
How did you know that?

                    JOCELYN
Same way you knew I wasn't from New York.

                    MAN
The travel bag with airline tags on it?

                    JOCELYN
What happened to primal feelings?

20

MAN

Sounded better than airline tags.

JOCELYN

I like you.

MAN

You don't know me.

JOCELYN

Who really knows anyone?

MAN

Are you goading me now? Because of the title of my book.

JOCELYN

I just always thought – the book's ideas only went so far.

MAN

On the contrary – they go deeper than most people who read it in high school can fathom.

JOCELYN

I read it in high school and then again in college. I think I fathomed it just fine.

MAN

When Marceau killed the Arab....why did he do that?

JOCELYN

He was angry because the Arab knifed a friend of his. He snapped.

MAN

That's exactly what someone who doesn't understand the book would say.

Marceau murders a man, not because of anything. The cause and effect is set up by Camus as a bait for our usual way of thinking. Nothing in the narrative suggests Marceau is angry. Marceau himself notes feeling more irritated by the heat and sun than by anything else. The murder is incidental, unimportant to him.

JOCELYN
That is just because he is disconnected even from himself.

MAN
Wrong. The book is about more than Marceau. It is about how we human beings try to make meaning out of everything that happens. Marceau murders someone....we try to explain it. Why? Because we are meaning-makers, which is absurd, since the world is meaningless. Marceau realizes that the world is meaningless, that his actions are no more profound or significant than a bolt of lightning randomly striking the man down. So he is not compelled to make meaning of his action. His action...like reality itself...is without meaning.

JOCELYN
But human beings don't work that way....

MAN
Well, that's true – but this is a parable about a human being who is perfectly aligned with a nihilistic view of life. If we truly grasped the meaninglessness of everything....we would be like Marceau. For instance, I could kiss you now and no one would freak out.

JOCELYN
I would.

MAN
Right, because you have to make meaning of everything. I would not, because I would understand it is as random as a gust of wind knocking a stray cat from a tree.

JOCELYN

If you think that is going to let me allow a stranger to kiss me...

MAN

I don't. I'm simply illustrating a point. Which is Marceau isn't trapped by the human folly of needing to make meaning of everything. Everyone else in the novel, the people at the trial, they need to interpret him as a monster, a soulless being, etc. but Marceau is just a true nihilist, a force of nature, totally random. It is not that he is unrepentant, or evil. It is that he just *is*. In the moment. Valueless, judgementless.

JOCELYN

He killed a man.

MAN

Morality is just a way for us to make meaning. This action is right. This one is wrong. Etc.

JOCELYN

Camus wouldn't even have the freedom to write his little book without morality. The world would be anarchy. He'd be fending off attackers with a stick.

MAN

Then people wouldn't need the book. They'd be more accurate to life. Random.

JOCELYN

Not random. The same reason he killed that man – human impulse. Those primal instincts you mentioned. The reason you said you wanted to kiss me.

MAN

Didn't say I wanted, was only illustrating a –

JOCELYN
(Jumping in to finish his sentence)
A subconscious primal desire to mate with an attractive member of
the same species. Are you saying Darwin was incorrect? That the
"meaning" science has made of the world should also be
disregarded as human folly?

MAN
I don't think Camus would say that... I mean.... that's applying his
ideas a bit out of scope....but if we want to go there... even the
"laws of nature" can be questioned... Intro to Philosophy - David
Hume.

JOCELYN
"How do you know", right? "How do you know the sun will rise
tomorrow? Just because it's risen every day before"? How do we
know the laws of nature we've observed today won't be gone
tomorrow?

MAN
Yes. Exactly. I mean, carbon dating shows things have been a
certain way for a very long time. But that very long time has been
the blink of an eye, really, on a cosmic level, so who knows how
consistent the universe really is....

JOCELYN
So what? We should just give up on trying to find meaning?

MAN
I'm just saying, if a random stranger kisses a woman he just met in
the Starbucks on 52nd Street, it doesn't have to be romantic. Or
weird and inappropriate. Or however you want to try and interpret
it....it can just *be.*

JOCELYN

Isn't science, putting things in order, morality, the unspoken rules of social engagement which specify we shouldn't kiss until we first get to know one another...isn't all of that keeping society in order and functioning – isn't it worthwhile....doesn't it make sense?

MAN

Making sense is the enemy of nihilism. Making sense is making meaning. And you cannot truly make meaning in a meaningless universe. In the end, it is a way to explain something beyond explanation. Not because that explanation really works – but because we need, we crave explanation. People kiss, they make love, they get married, they have kids. Why? Because they love each other? No. Because things happen. Things without explanation. But we people, we want to understand why. We want to make meaning. But there is none. There is no meaning to make. We crave it, so we invent it. We invent explanations and we think we understand ourselves. But, really, we just need to understand. So we make up pretty lies that help us sleep better at night.

JOCELYN

So where does that leave us? I mean, if we accept meaninglessness ...why even live life?

MAN

Well...in the end of the book Marceau realizes the value of life. Realizes that, despite its meaninglessness, it is worth living. Sensation, feeling, pleasure. It is of value. Life is of value.

JOCELYN

Why wouldn't that realization make him feel repentant that he stole someone's?

MAN

He's not so narrow minded that he needs to find meaning in his actions in order to find value in his life.

JOCELYN

Look, if he really gave up on meaning....he wouldn't be able to put two coherent thoughts together. So let's say we humans are wrong about 99% of everything. We're obviously right about some things, because we get out of bed, brush our teeth –

MAN

- send rockets into space using physics.

JOCELYN

Yes. Thank you. Yes.

MAN

So we are right about a few things.

JOCELYN

Physics give us meaning. They prove there is a meaning to be found, explained. Things can be predicted and explained.

MAN

Laws that could change tomorrow.

JOCELYN

But for now they work. We follow them. We live. We survive.

MAN

Back to Darwin.

JOCELYN

We're here – in this Starbucks on 52nd Street - because our ancestors made meaning better than others. Understood and adapted to their environment better than others.

MAN

Maybe we're here because our ancestors were simply in the right places at the right times.

Avoided large wars, famines, plagues, and natural disasters. Our existence is incidental, random change.

JOCELYN

Probably some percentage of both.

MAN

Maybe we're just here because we both like caffeine.

JOCELYN

That's the first sensible thing you've said. I'm Jocelyn.

MAN

Jocelyn Beard?

JOCELYN

The editor of monologue books. No.

MAN

I knew it! Theatre major! Tisch?

JOCELYN

The sticker on my bag.

MAN

Yeah....so not Jocelyn Beard.

JOCELYN

But if you think I'm giving you my last name so you can find me on Google, follow me on Twitter, and friend me on Facebook, you've got another thing coming. So you know the name Jocelyn Beard. You go to Tisch?

                              MAN
I did. Switched my major.

                            JOCELYN
Philosophy.

                              MAN
How did you guess?

                            JOCELYN
Last five minutes of pseudo-intellectual drivel.

                              MAN
Well...I'm thinking of switching my major again to social psychology.

                            JOCELYN
What would Camus say?

                              MAN
Study the folly of humans. He'd like it. But I'm almost over this
phase, I think. Of loving Camus.

                            JOCELYN
You were a passionate advocate when I met you.

                              MAN
I think you've changed my mind. Almost.

                            JOCELYN
What would change your mind fully?

                              MAN
Well...I would be willing to interpret it as romantic....if something
happened here.

JOCELYN

So kind. I'll tell you what. I have a class Wednesdays, this Starbucks will be conducive to after-class lunches on that day....

MAN

So, like, a regular date?

JOCELYN

That doesn't require a last name or exchange of phone numbers.

MAN

Seal the deal with a kiss...

JOCELYN

I really don't know you yet.

MAN

Yes, but don't you think that...kissing me as a stranger is going to be far more exhilarating than kissing me later when you actually know me? I mean, why waste this?

JOCELYN

Several reasons. Including that herpes is communicable by kissing.

MAN

That is a fair point. Nevertheless, if you scrutinize me carefully, you will note a healthy hue to my face and lips..
        (He leans toward her, offering his lips)

JOCELYN

Ha ha, that is funny. Are you just going to stay leaned over the table like that until I what? Lean in and kiss you?

MAN

That's the plan, yes.

JOCELYN
Then hold that pose.... I will see you next time.

(She moves away from the table)

MAN
Goodbye, Jocelyn Beard.

JOCELYN
Goodbye... stranger.

END OF PLAY

Anniversary

5 Minute Play

By Gabriel Davis

gabriel@alumni.cmu.edu
gabrielbdavis.com

Cast
1 w, 1 m

Characters
Stephen
Anne

Both characters are in their late thirties to early forties.

Time & Setting
Present day. A hotel suite.

(Anne enters, frazzled)

ANNE

Hi, sorry, sorry...I tried to call but it went straight to voicemail.

STEPHEN

Andrew grabbed my cell during his bath time last night...hasn't been working right—

ANNE

Wow, Stephen. Nice room.

STEPHEN

It's a suite.

ANNE

Sweet suite.

STEPHEN

Sit, I poured some bubbly for us.

ANNE

Thanks. I'm so sorry—

STEPHEN

Don't be. Let's toast.
        (Stephen hands Anne a glass, and raises his)
To our anniversary.

ANNE

Anniversary?

STEPHEN

It's been one year as of today.

                              ANNE
Anniversaries are for married people.

                           STEPHEN
We're married people.

                              ANNE
Funny.

                           STEPHEN
         (Laughing)
You to Eric, me to Ally. C'mon. Let's toast – to one year of
decadent sin!

         (Anne doesn't raise her glass)

                              ANNE
I would have been here sooner—

                           STEPHEN
It's ok.

                              ANNE
--but Jules is scared of the new sitter.

                           STEPHEN
The one Ally and I recommended?

                              ANNE
Uh-huh. Apparently Jules found out this woman is of German
descent– and you know, they're learning about the Holocaust now
in school and...

                           STEPHEN
         (Laughing)
Your daughter thinks the sitter is a Nazi?

ANNE

It's not funny. Your son is the one who told Jules she's German.

STEPHEN

How does Andrew know that?

ANNE

I don't know, but he told Jules this, and she's freaking out, ok.

STEPHEN

Ok. We going to toast? This is a hundred dollar bottle of—

ANNE

I keep wondering why he would tell Jules that. Did he want to scare her?

STEPHEN

Do we really want to spend our time talking about our kids?

ANNE

Why? How long do we have?

STEPHEN

We're fine—Ally thinks I'm staying in DC tonight—

ANNE

Good. I mean, not good but...

STEPHEN

Yes, good. Let's celebrate. To our anniversary.

ANNE

That's kind of sick. Calling it an anniversary.

STEPHEN

Come here. Let's work some of that tension out.
     (He starts rubbing her shoulders)

ANNE

Oh, nice. A little to the left. Oh yeah. Right there. Right...wait.
     (Jules stops, pulls out her cell)

STEPHEN

What's wrong?

ANNE

No, I thought I felt it vibrating – I don't want to miss it if the sitter
calls—I told her she could if Jules started to freak again—

STEPHEN

She'll be fine.

ANNE

I don't know, Stephen. She's been playing this disturbing game at
school—actually Andrew's involved too....

STEPHEN

What are you talking about?

ANNE

I guess it's because of what they're learning in school but—Andrew
and Jules have been playing Holocaust at recess.

STEPHEN

What?

ANNE

It's like a game of tag – but sick.

Apparently one child plays Hitler—and this child assigns people, some of the other bigger kids on the playground to be his SS officers and they chase the other smaller kids the "prisoners" around the playground and when they catch them, those kids have to go stand and wait in an area dubbed the gas chamber. And every time, apparently Jules is made to play a prisoner and the other day, Andrew was assigned as an SS officer and he had to catch my daughter. And he did. Your son sent my daughter to the gas chamber in recess yesterday!!

STEPHEN
I'm sure he was just following orders.

ANNE
That's not funny. Stephen, she's scared of Andrew now.

STEPHEN
Scared of—those two love each other, Anne. I think I—I think I know what this is...I think Andrew tried to tell me about it.

ANNE
He did?

STEPHEN
It was about two days ago?

ANNE
Uh huh.

STEPHEN
Uh huh. Andrew didn't tell me exactly what it was but he was upset and I could just tell something was— that he was troubled about something—

So I asked and he said one of the bigger kids made him play a mean game at recess. I kinda gathered from his descriptions it was a game of tag of some kind, so, yes, it must be the same thing and....but he said he only played so he wouldn't get picked on himself. He felt so ashamed.

                    ANNE
Good.

                    STEPHEN
Good?

                    ANNE
He was victimizing other kids, Stephen.

                    STEPHEN
They all were; it was just—it was a bad game they were all sort of trapped in. He was as much a victim.

                    ANNE
Oh please. He was playing an SS officer. The other children—the prisoners—were the victims.

                    STEPHEN
Is it that black and white to you?

                    ANNE
Yes.

                    STEPHEN
Anne, I told him, I said, he shouldn't feel ashamed. That sometimes we do things we're not proud of, because we have to, because the alternative—

                    ANNE
You're apologizing for his behavior?

STEPHEN

No, I'm—and they're not, they're kids—I'm just saying—a child giving in to peer pressure—from what he said, the other kids were pushing kids down, I mean, really being brutal. And some of the kids, the prisoners, who were being chased, some of them were pushing each other down to escape getting tagged, hard into the concrete, skinned knees and…. I mean, for crying out loud, where were the teachers… I mean, it sounded really brutal. And I asked him, I said, did you actually push or shove anyone? And he said—he said no, Anne. He didn't. He tagged people, as few as he could without getting noticed and he tagged them lightly. He tried to be as gentle as he could. But what else could he do? If he didn't tag the other kids and he did it lightly—they'd have pushed him down, injured him. So you know what? I'm glad. I'm glad he kept his head down and went along – he survived. My son's a survivor and I don't want him to feel ashamed of that.

ANNE

I cannot believe you.

STEPHEN

And he said Jules pushed a kid down.

ANNE

What?

STEPHEN

He said your daughter, in trying to escape getting tagged pushed other children down and even flung other children into the aggressors. But he's the victimizer? He's the one should feel ashamed?

ANNE

Yes, he should have refused to play.

STEPHEN

That's a fairly moral stance to take.

ANNE

Yes...it is.
>   (Anne stands up and moves to leave)

STEPHEN

Where are you going? It's our anniversary.

ANNE

That's sick, Stephen.
>   (Ann exits. Stephen, alone in the room, raises his glass.)

STEPHEN

Happy Anniversary.
>   (He drinks, lights fade to black)

END OF PLAY

Printed in Great Britain
by Amazon